Dear Parent:
Your child's love of reading starts here!

Every child learns to read in a different way and at his or her own speed. You can help your young reader improve and become more confident by encouraging his or her own interests and abilities. You can also guide your child's spiritual development by reading stories with biblical values and Bible stories, like I Can Read! books published by Zonderkidz. From books your child reads with you to the first books he or she reads alone, there are I Can Read! books for every stage of reading:

SHARED READING
Basic language, word repetition, and whimsical illustrations, ideal for sharing with your emergent reader.

BEGINNING READING
Short sentences, familiar words, and simple concepts for children eager to read on their own.

READING WITH HELP
Engaging stories, longer sentences, and language play for developing readers.

READING ALONE
Complex plots, challenging vocabulary, and high-interest topics for the independent reader.

ADVANCED READING
Short paragraphs, chapters, and exciting themes for the perfect bridge to chapter books.

I Can Read! books have introduced children to the joy of reading since 1957. Featuring award-winning authors and illustrators and a fabulous cast of beloved characters, I Can Read! books set the standard for beginning readers.

A lifetime of discovery begins with the magical words **"I Can Read!"**

Visit www.icanread.com for information on enriching your child's reading experience.
Visit www.zonderkidz.com for more Zonderkidz I Can Read! titles.

Then God said, "Let us make mankind in our image, in our likeness, so that they may rule over the fish in the sea and the birds in the sky, over the livestock and all the wild animals, and over all the creatures that move along the ground."

—Genesis 1:26

ZONDERKIDZ

Barnyard Critters
Copyright © 2011 by Zonderkidz

Requests for information should be addressed to:
Zonderkidz, *Grand Rapids, Michigan 49530*

Library of Congress Cataloging-in-Publication Data

Barnyard critters.
     p. cm.
  ISBN 978-0-310-72189-5 (softcover)
  1. Livestock—Religious aspects—Christianity—Juvenile literature. 2. Creation—Juvenile literature.
  BT746.B38 2011
  231.7–dc22   2010029693

Editor: *Mary Hassinger*
Art direction: *Jody Langley*

Printed in China

11 12 13 14 15 16 17 /SCC/ 10 9 8 7 6 5 4 3 2 1

MADE · BY · GOD

Barnyard Critters

CONTENTS

God made all creatures.

He made wild animals that live

in jungles.

He made tame animals too.

Some live in our homes.

Others live on farms

and are called livestock, like …

COWS!

Cows live in herds.

Fathers are called bulls.

Mothers are called cows.

Baby cows are called calves.
Cows carry their babies for
nine months before giving birth.
A bull can grow up to weigh
an amazing 3,000 pounds!

Meat from cows is called beef.

Burgers and steaks are beef.

We use cowhides for leather

to make clothing, shoes, and belts.

Dairy cows are milked twice a day.

We drink milk and use it to make

cheese, yogurt, and ice cream!

We can also use cows to pull things
on a farm, like plows and carts.
We use their manure to help
plants grow.

Cattle do something gross!

They eat food, swallow it,

spit it back up, chew it,

and swallow it again.

This is called chewing their cud.

God made another animal on the farm

that chews their cud, the …

GOAT!

Like cows, goats have special
stomachs with four parts.
Goats are curious.
They like to taste everything
but are fussy about what they eat.

Goats come in many colors.

Most goats have horns, beards,

and short hair.

Billy goats are smelly!

This is because of a spot

on their head called a musk gland.

Goats live all over the world.
People drink their milk, eat their
meat, and use their hair and hide.

15

Goats are also great pets!

They are friendly and smart.

Goats can be trained to walk on a leash.

Mother goats are called does or nannies.

Father goats are called bucks or billies.

Baby goats are called kids.

Mothers often give birth

to twins or triplets.

God made all farm animals,

and he made them all good, like the …

PIG!

Pigs have a snout for a nose,

and a small, curly or straight tail.

They have a big body and short legs.

Most pigs have four toes on each foot.

They walk on the two middle toes.

The other toes help them balance.

Pigs are clean animals.

They do not like to make a mess

where they eat or sleep.

But pigs do not sweat.

They cool off by rolling in water

or mud during the summer.

The mud helps a pig not get sunburn.

Mud also keeps away flies.

Pigs are omnivores.

They eat meat and plants.

Unlike cattle and goats,
pigs must chew their food well
the first time they eat it.

They have 44 teeth to help them.

Mother pigs are called sows.

Father pigs are called boars.

Baby pigs are called piglets.

A group of piglets is called a litter.

Sows have 6–12 piglets in a litter.

Pig meat is called pork.

Bacon and ham are pork.

The rough hair of a pig

is used for brushes.

It has been said that every part

of a pig is useful but the "oink!"

God created farm animals
big and small.
Some have hair and
others have feathers, like the …

CHICKEN!

Chickens are a kind of bird.

They are also called poultry.

There are thousands of kinds of

chickens all over the world!

Chickens provide eggs and meat to eat.

Mother chickens are called hens.

Father chickens are called roosters.

Chickens live in groups called flocks.

Babies are called chicks.

Hens sit on their eggs until they hatch after 21 days.

Chickens have a red crest of skin
on their heads called a comb.
On their chins are red wattles,
which help keep them cool.
Roosters have sharp spurs
on their heels for fighting.

Chicken feathers are many amazing colors and patterns.

Like pigs, chickens are omnivores. They can catch and eat mice.

They scratch at the ground to look for plants, seeds, and bugs to eat.

Chickens live in houses called coops.

Coops protect them at night

when other animals, like red foxes,

raccoons, and coyotes, hunt them.

Coops have boxes to lay eggs in

and roosts to stand on.

God blessed us with farms filled
with wonderful and useful animals.
If we care for them,
they will give us much!